How To INSTALL KODI ON FIRE STICK

Step-By-Step Instructions With Screenshots!

By
Steve Wright

WHY YOU NEED THIS BOOK

This book is written for those who are puzzled by the Kodi. Are you one who is not that tech savvy but wants to take advantage of Kodi? This book will help you setup Kodi on Firestick and start using it within minutes. Install your favourite game or watch the latest Soccer Live on your TV. Are you ready to be amazed by the magic of Kodi? Read on and find why the world is going one step smarter with Kodi.

Welcome to your SMART LIFE!

Amazon Fire TV Stick is a powerful media-streaming player. With this smart device you can now enjoy over 7,000 apps, games, and Alexa skills including Netflix, HBO NOW, Amazon Video, YouTube, NBC, Disney and much more. No cable or satellite? No problem. Watch the best of live TV and sports or top-rated primetime shows. Using the universal search results you can search for the best of entertainment from over 100 channels and apps including Hulu, Netflix and Amazon Video. What more...bring hit shows and movies with you when you travel. Plug Fire TV Stick into any TV's HDMI port, connect to Wi-Fi, and continue watching.

But using the Amazon Fire TV/Stick can be an expensive proposition in the long term. You may end up spending hundreds of dollars each month to access the best of entertainment. This is where Kodi comes in.

Kodi is a free and open-source media player developed by XBMC foundation. It allows users to play and view most streaming media, such as videos, music, podcasts, and videogames from the internet, as well as all common digital media files from local and network storage media. With the help of hundreds of add-ons you can easily stream you favorite Movie, TV show or music for cheaper or even free. Plus it also integrates with your personal media files and enables you to watch your stores content on your TV.

This book is written from my personal experience and anecdotal evidence from hundreds of fellow Kodi Users who have helped me adapt this smart player into my life. Through this book, my goal is to help you setup Kodi on your Amazon Fire TV stick and start using it like a pro.

After reading this book you will be able to

- Install Kodi and start using it on your Firestick
- Install Add-ons on Kodi to watch your favorite programs for free or watch Live TV
- Integrate all your personal media files with Kodi and what them on your Big Screen TV

So, let's begin the journey to discover how to install and use Kodi to its best advantage.

TABLE OF CONTENTS

INTRODUCTION

Amazon Fire Stick and Fire TV are two devices by Amazon to change the way you use your television. They enhance your television so that you can use it to play games and use it for streaming services such as Netflix. Both of these devices differ only in hardware, and since the Fire TV is more expensive it has certain added features.

Kodi is an external application that does not come pre-installed with Fire Stick or TV. It is a digital software interface that allows users to play any kind of digital content, such as music, movies, TV shows and even local media, from storage. Kodi is all that you need to take your Fire Stick and TV experience to the next level.

Installing Kodi can be a bit of a hassle since it's not an application that is officially supported by Amazon, but with a little tinkering, you can install it quickly. This book has detailed instructions that are given in a clear and concise manner to explain the installation and use of Kodi.

This book has been written in a simplistic manner to explain the complex functioning of Amazon Fire Stick and TV as well as Kodi. Even if you have some prior knowledge about the intricacies of this topic, you will still find some useful tips and tricks to augment your experience.

Thank you for buying this book and I hope that it answers all your queries.

CHAPTER 1:

WHAT IS KODI ?

Kodi is a free and open source media center platform that allows you to aggregate all of your various media sources and streams into one, easy to navigate, source. The fact that it is open source means that anyone is free to develop new add-ons for the program, which in turn means that the program's utility will continually improve.

Kodi is a media platform, which allows the Fire Stick and TV to be more versatile than the traditional interface that usually comes with the Fire Stick and TV. The concept of add-ons allows Kodi to be modified so that different kind of programs can be used with it. Essentially, Kodi is a media hub, which can easily replace the original interface of your Smart TV and enhance your user experience.

The highly popular media center app allows you to not only access all of your personal media, but it also helps you integrate subscriptions to various media websites, integrate photos from nationally known papers, and even add on foreign news services.

In the following chapters, you will learn about Kodi and all its features. You will discover what makes Kodi the preferred media player and open source cross-platform for millions of users. More importantly, you will also learn several methods to install Kodi onto your Amazon Fire TV so that you can begin to enjoy all the features that Kodi has to offer.

Origins of Kodi

Kodi is the free alternative to Windows Media Center. It was introduced in 2002 as an Xbox Media Player and has since grown into a multi-platform open-source media player. Originally developed by the XBMC Foundation, this media player allowed Xbox owners to use their Xboxes as more than just game systems. They could now display pictures, watch movies or play music, which made having to own or purchase additional devices such as CD players, stereos, and DVD players an obsolete concept.

From its beginnings, Kodi has never stopped adapting to the latest media available. It has been developed and redesigned over the years. It has grown from a simple multimedia platform of a gaming system to a multimedia platform for all electronics. Personal devices using Kodi are now capable of accessing streaming, stored, live, and digital media. Once it was only compatible with Xbox, but now it is almost universally compatible with nearly every operating system in the world. Over the years, it has been known by many names, but the core function of this amazing media player has never changed much and continues to allow the consumer access to media, weather, news and much more in any version they desire from live to stored sources.

Kodi is compatible with numerous operating systems, including Microsoft Windows, Mac and IOC. Kodi allows users to stream the media of their choice, such as podcasts, music and videos from a variety of sources, such as the Internet or network storage. It can be personalized to suit the user's preferences and the available plug-ins make access to media content easy. Pandora, Spotify, YouTube and Amazon Prime all have plug-ins available for Kodi.

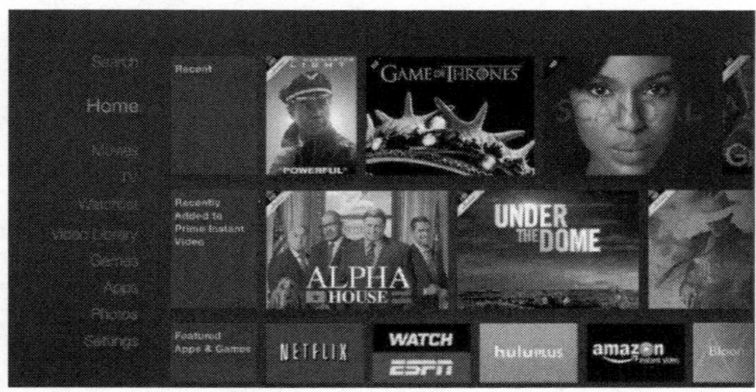

The software for Kodi is always being updated and the latest additions include video recording capabilities that are a compliment to existing features such as weather, slideshows, audio, game launching, and video. It can be used with multiple devices including Smartphones, tablets, computers, and televisions. For your added convenience you can also use your phone or tablet as a remote control.

Before you install Kodi there are a few key pieces of information that you may want to know about this media player. Kodi has not always been Kodi. You may be more familiar with this open source media center by its former name, XBMC. Kodi is over a decade old. Kodi began as Xbox Media Player in 2002, before becoming Xbox Media Center in 2003.

In its original version, it was developed to act as a media platform for the original, first-generation Xbox game console. Kodi is always in the development stage and the nonprofit consortium of developers is always tweaking and perfecting Kodi. Even though there is an official version and it has been tested and released to millions, it will be followed by a new more improved version in the future that is probably already in the works. 60 developers work on Kodi on an ongoing and continuous basis.

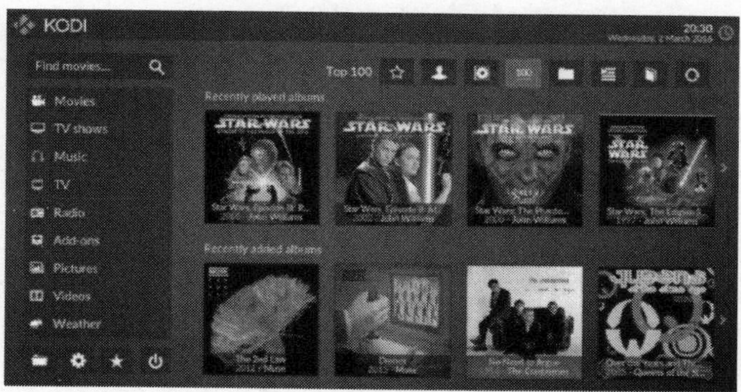

Kodi was developed as a nonprofit software. Kodi is managed by the XBMC Foundation, which is listed as a nonprofit organization. It has been developed by over 500 volunteers since its origin in 2002.

The latest version of Kodi is known as Kodi 17.0. (Krypton) and is compatible with all major operating systems. It comes with many under-the-hood changes to settings and a new interface that increases the operating efficiency of the application.

A new skin, named Estuary, has been specifically designed for this version of Kodi, which adds to the aesthetic value of the application. The Audio and Visuals settings have been tweaked and you can actually see the change while playing videos and music. Other than that, this version also comes with certain specific settings that add to the compatibility of the software with Amazon Fire.

CHAPTER 2:

WHY INSTALL KODI ON FIRE STICK ?

The Amazon Fire Stick is a small device that looks like a USB drive and it can fit into your TV's HDMI port. It is essentially a replacement for a Smart TV because Smart TV's can be really expensive and not everyone can buy them. So, you can turn your regular TV into a Smart TV by using Fire Stick, which enables your TV to access stream services such as Netflix, Hulu or Amazon Prime over the Internet. It basically connects your TV to streaming services so that you can watch your favorite shows or movies on your TV. The combination of Fire Stick + Kodi just takes your home theatre experience to the next level.

The Fire TV, on the other hand, is slightly more expensive and has different hardware. The Fire TV comes with a small box that you have to connect to your Smart TV just like the Stick. It has added features along with better resolution and sound quality and will give you a better viewing experience than the Fire Stick.

Fire Stick/TV Features

Powerful Streaming

Amazon Fire has a great RAM and a fluid dual-processor that enables you to stream at the speed of light. You don't have to worry about efficiency as your Fire Stick or TV will never lag or make you wait while the content buffers. The Fire Stick's processor has been designed to handle a huge amount of activity so you can use it for days without experiencing any kind of problem.

Voice Search

The Fire Stick and TV come packed with voice search that actually works, so you can configure your TV just by just using your voice. If you know what you want to watch, but don't want to make an effort to find it, all you have to do it speak into your phone and the Fire Stick or TV will find what you're looking for. You can sort between thousands of episodes or movies by using advanced search options, such as filter by actors, genres and ratings.

Content

The one thing that you will never lack in once you buy the Amazon Fire is content. It gives you access to over 4,000 streaming services, channels, apps and games. You can even find the latest music or play your favorite games. And, with Kodi installed, you can access any and every kind of content from all over the globe.

Amazon even gives you the option to rent movies at just 99 cents and you can also watch live TV. If you want to watch your favorite Football match on ESPN then you can do so with the help of Sling TV, which is part of the Fire Stick. Don't want to spend a cent renting movies? No problem, install Kodi addons and find your favorite movie online.

Voice Search and Controls

You can focus on more on watching than dealing with the controls with the Fire TV remote app. You can find the app on Google Play or the Apple Store and it'll help you to control your TV by just using your voice. It can be difficult to use the Fire remote because you have to type everything. Typing takes a lot of time and it can be quite annoying for a lot of people who are not used to typing on a regular basis. Using the Fire TV Voice app can solve this problem. This aap allows users to search for shows and give instructions by just speaking.

If you want to open Netflix, all you have to say is "Open Netflix" and your work is done. You can even control the content that is playing on your TV by giving instructions to the app. You can say "Stop" or "Pause" and you will see the result automatically on your TV. It's really intriguing because you feel like you are using a TV from the future.

Screen sharing and display mirroring

Screen sharing and display mirroring are two ways that you can put whatever is on your phone or tablet screen on your TV. If you are with the family or want the whole room to watch something then just use screen sharing to show whatever is on your phone screen on your TV. You can even play music, videos or movies on your other electronic devices and they will appear on your TV screen.

Less Buffering

Fire does not completely remove buffering, but it considerably reduces it. Amazon came up with a technology known as ASAP (advanced streaming and predicting); it's a smart software, which predicts the kind of shows or movies that you're likely to watch and keeps them ready. So, if you go to sleep at night after watching 5 episodes of your favorite show, the Fire Stick will buffer the rest of the episodes automatically.

The software becomes more accurate as you start to use your Fire Stick or TV more and at some point, it will correctly predict almost every one of your picks. It's quite outstanding and saves a lot of time, as you don't have to wait for buffering.

CHAPTER 3:

INSTALL KODI ON FIRE STICK

Taking advantage of the many great features and capabilities of Kodi starts with Amazon Fire TV. Amazon Fire offers the best option for utilizing Kodi on your television. Installation is quick and Kodi is highly compatible with Amazon Fire. Kodi can be installed in only a few minutes in just a few simple steps by using any number of methods including the side load method.

Although any of the methods available are quick and only require a few steps, many users prefer the side load method. Side loading is similar to uploading or downloading but is seen as a shortcut or bypass to the more conventional methods of installing an application.

This method does not require modification or require the user to root your Amazon Fire TV. The side load method can be used for Amazon Fire TV or Fire Stick TV.

Kodi can be installed using several methods and many of these methods are based on side loading, which does not require additional or advanced hardware.

Kodi can be installed to Amazon Fire TV using apps available in Google Play and that are available for download on Kodi's website, Kodi.tv. Using the apps makes installation simple and easy. In this book, you will discover several methods that will have Kodi installed in your Amazon Fire TV in just minutes.

Methods of Installation

There are many methods for installing Kodi onto a Fire Stick. If you are using Fire TV, it uses Kodi for android and does not require root. As mentioned earlier, Amazon Fire TV products allow users to side load Kodi.

Before installing Kodi on your Amazon Fire Stick, it is important to understand that the official version of Kodi has absolutely no content. Kodi functions as a media player and does not have any content. All content must be provided by a local or remote storage location, a media carrier, DVDs, Blu-ray, etc. Content can also be provided by the access you can receive by installing additional plug-ins available from third parties. These plugins will allow you access to content that is available for free from websites that offer content.

Now lets explore the different methods outlined for installing

Kodi. These different methods allow you to access Kodi and to install it using different techniques depending on the equipment that you have available. Each of these techniques works equally well and will help you to Install Kodi in minutes.

Method #1 is the easiest and the most straight-forward technique. Here you are using the ES file explorer app on your Fire Stick/TV to install Kodi. This method does not need any other device or your computer and you can access Kodi within minutes.

Method #2 and Method #3 are a bit more complicated in that it requires you to use your android phone/tablet device to sideload the Kodi on an App and then intall it on your Fire Stick/TV. But I promise that its will take may be a few more minutes or sometimes even less. But the advantage is that you can use these Apps to load Addons and access media on your Kodi.

Installing Kodi onto an Amazon Fire TV or Fire Stick is easy just start with the directions listed below.

Method #4 is for those who are more comfortable using their computer to install Kodi on their Fire devices or those who do not have an android mobile device.

Method #1: Using ES File Explorer on Your Fire Stick or Fire TV Device

This is one of the simplest methods of installing KODI on your Amazon Fire Stick or Fire TV. Basically, you will need to download the ES File Explorer App on your Amazon Fire device and use that to install KODI on your device. Since Amazon doesn't have the KODI app in its store, this is a quick hack one can use to Install KODI fast.

Detailed Description

Step#1: Hardware Setup

- The first thing to do is to make sure your Fire TV Stick is plugged into the HDMI port into your TV.
- Set it up as normal with your Amazon account.

Step#2: Turn ON the <u>Apps from Unknown Sources</u> feature in your Fire Device

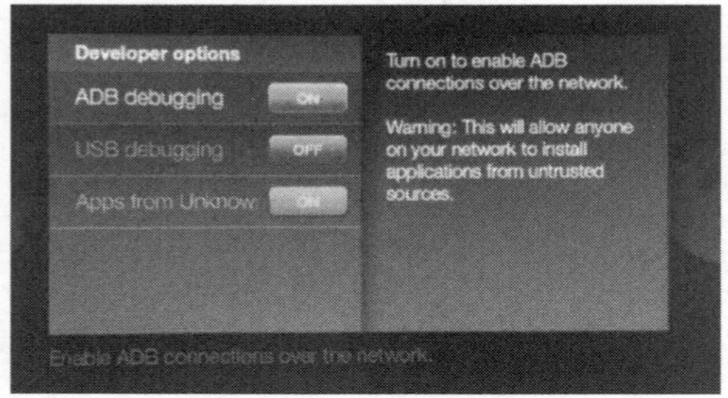

- Go to Main Menu on the Left Hand Side
- Tap **<u>Settings</u>**
- Inside Settings Tap **<u>System</u>**
- Inside System Tap **<u>Developer Options</u>**
- Enable **<u>ADB Debugging</u>** and **<u>Apps from Unknown Sources</u>**

Step#3: Turn OFF <u>Collect App Usage Data</u> feature

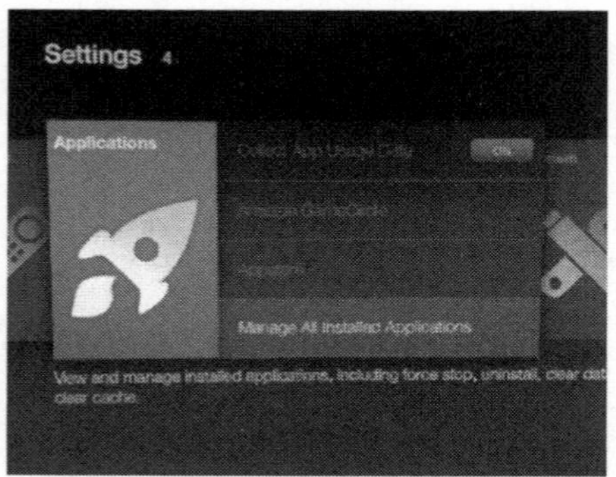

- Go to Main Menu on the Left Hand Side
- Tap **Settings**
- Inside Settings Tap **Applications**
- Disable **Collect App Usage Data**

Step#4: Download and Install the ES File Explorer App

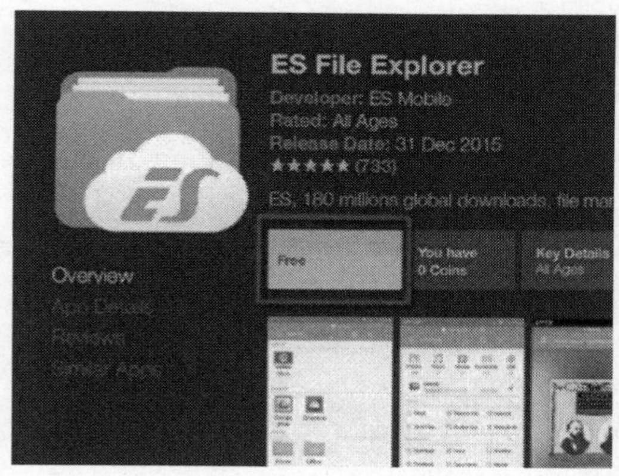

- Use your search box on the Fire home screen to find **ES File Explorer**
- Tap on the icon to **download** the App
- **Launch** the ES File Explorer App

Step#5: Download and Install the KODI

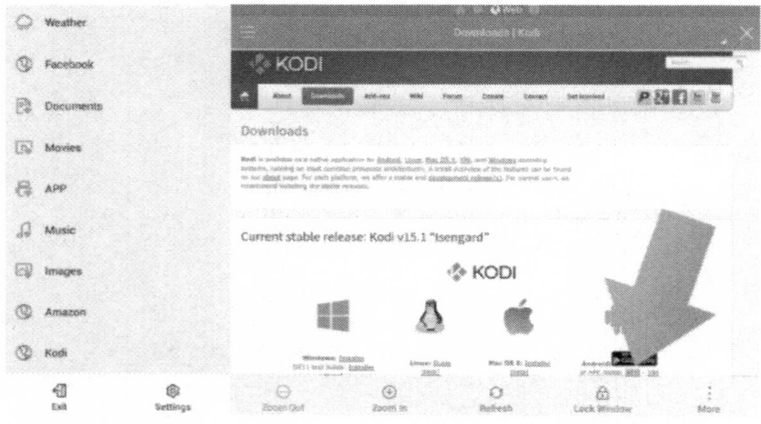

- Open up the **ES File Explorer app**
- Go to **Menu** on left hand side
- Click on the **add(+)** button
- Now it will ask you to add the **PATH** and the **NAME**
- On the keypad type the **PATH** as **http:\\kodi.tv\download**
- On the keypad type the **NAME** as **Kodi**
- Tap **Add**
- Now you can see the **Kodi** bookmark in the Menu
- Tap on the **Kodi** bookmark, it will take you to the Kodi website
- On the website, you can see various download options for Kodi
- Tap on the **Android APK ARM** option to **download** Kodi
- Once the download is complete, Tap **Install**
- Now you can **Open** Kodi and commence your media consolidation

Method #2: Cetus Play App on Android Device

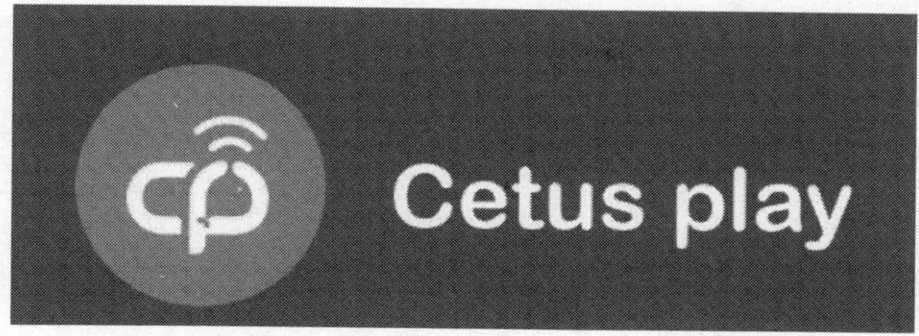

This is the latest method that allows you to side load Kodi and other popular apps to Fire TV from your android phone/tablet. If you have and Android mobile device, this is the best Kodi installation method hands down. It's a virtually 1-click method plus you get auto update wherever a new Kodi version is launched.

This method allows the user the option of using the remote function for your Fire TV using the Cetus Platy App. The first step in this method is to install the Cetus Play app from Google Play on your phone. Next, enable the developer settings on your Fire TV and be sure to enable the ADB on the Fire TV. Once this is enabled there will be a TV server of Cetus Play automatically installed on your TV. On the App Center in Cetus Play, select Kodi from the top of the list and clock Install to finish this method.

Detailed Description

Step#1: Hardware Setup

- The first thing to do is to make sure your Fire TV Stick is plugged into the HDMI port into your TV.
- Set it up as normal with your Amazon account.
- Make sure your Fire TV Stick is connected to the **same router** as your phone or tablet.

Step#2: Turn ON the <u>Apps from Unknown Sources</u> feature

- Go to Main Menu on the Left Hand Side
- Tap **<u>Settings</u>**
- Inside Settings Tap **<u>System</u>**
- Inside System Tap **<u>Developer Options</u>**
- Enable **<u>ADB Debugging</u>** and **<u>Apps from Unknown Sources</u>**

Step#3: Find the <u>IP address</u> of your Amazon Firestick/TV

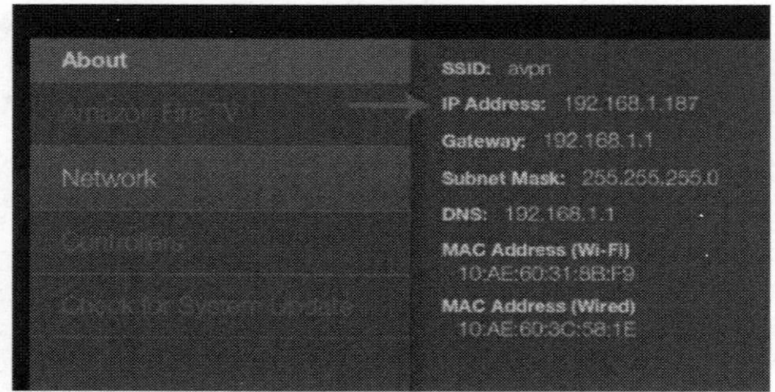

- Inside System Tap **<u>About</u>**
- Inside About Tap **<u>Network</u>**
- Here you can see the **<u>IP Address</u>** for your device
- Note down this address as we are going to use it later.

Step#4: Download and install the <u>CetusPlay Remote & Sideload App</u> on your android phone/tablet

- Ensure that you are using the same **<u>same router</u>** as your Fire device

- Bring up the Google Play Store on your phone or tablet
- Search for and install the **CetusPlay Remote & Sideload App** on your device
- Open up the CetusPlay app, on the top right hand corner tap on **Smart TV**
- Now you can see **New Devices** on this page with a list of devices to connect.
- Select the **Fire TV** from among the list and tap on **Connect**
- Wait for a few seconds and check your TV screen, on the bottom left hand corner it will it will notify **"CetusPlay For TV has connected"**
- Next you can see a **4-digit code** appear on your TV screen. Feed this code on your phone/tablet.
- Now, you can remote control your Fire TV device using the CetusPlay App.

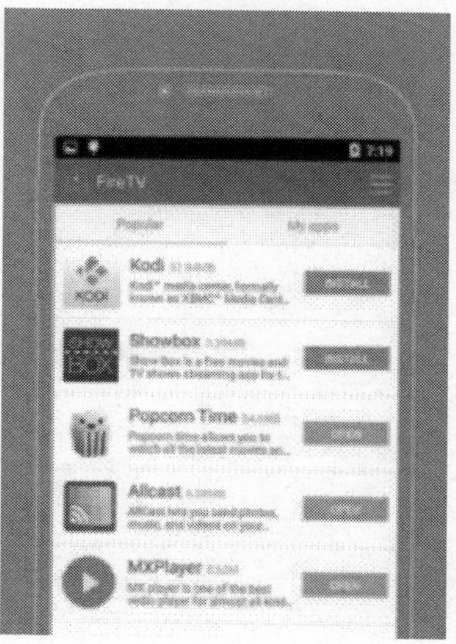

Step#4: Download and install the Kodi App on your CetusPlay App

- Go to the App Store in your CetusPlay App on the bottom left hand corner.
- It will show you a list of Apps you can download. Find the Kodi App from the List and tap Install.
- You can see a **Installing Kodi** notification on your TV screen. A page with an **Install** option will come up.
- Next, use your CetusPlay App remote to tap Install on your

TV Screen.

- Now Kodi will be installed. Tap **<u>Open</u>** using the CetusPlay App remote or your Fire Stick remote and commence your media consolidation

Sometimes, you will get an error notification **"cannot download obb"** as soon as you try to open the Kodi app after installation. The solution is to download a game/app over 50mb on your Amazon fire device, this will install the obb file you need to open the Kodi on your firestick.

Method #3: Using Apps2fire app On Your Android Device

Apps2fire is very versatile and can run from any android phone or tablet. The phone or tablet that had apps2fire has the ability to install apps to the Fire TV Box or Fire TV stick. To begin KODI installation make sure that your phone or tablet is connected to the same network as the Fire TV.

Detailed Description

Step#1: Hardware Setup

- The first thing to do is to make sure your Fire TV Stick is plugged into the HDMI port into your TV.
- Set it up as normal with your Amazon account.
- Make sure your Fire TV Stick is connected to the **same router** as your phone or tablet.

Step#2: Turn ON the Apps from Unknown Sources feature

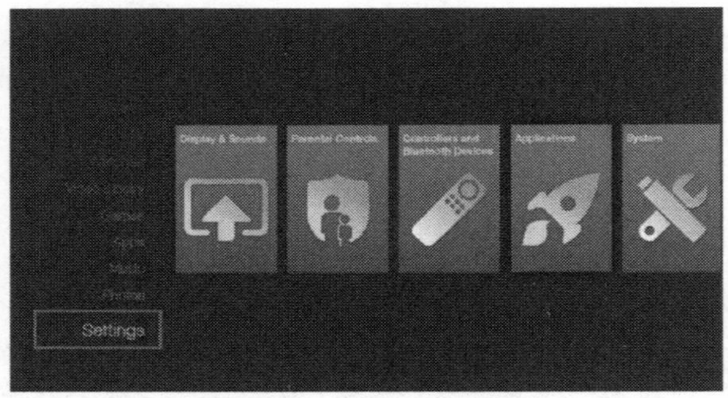

- Go to Main Menu on the Left Hand Side
- Tap **Settings**
- Inside Settings Tap **System**
- Inside System Tap **Developer Options**
- Enable **ADB Debugging** and **Apps from Unknown Sources**

Step#3: Find the IP address of your Amazon Firestick/TV

- Inside System Tap **About**
- Inside About Tap **Network**
- Here you can see the **IP Address** for your device
- Note down this address as we are going to use it later

Step#4: Turn OFF Collect App Usage Data feature

- Go to Main Menu on the Left Hand Side
- Tap **Settings**
- Inside Settings Tap **Applications**
- Disable **Collect App Usage Data**

Step#5: Install Apps2fire and Kodi on your Android Device

- Ensure that you are using the same **same router** as your Fire device
- Bring up the Google Play Store on your phone or tablet
- Search for and install **apps2fire** and **Kodi** on your device
- Open up apps2fire and go to **Setup**
- Type in the **IP address** that you got in Step#3 and it will connect your fire device to your android device
- Go to the **Local Apps** button on your apps2fire app
- Scroll down the list and install **Kodi**. This will install Kodi on your Fire device.
- Go to your Fire Device and search for the installed kodi app
- Now you can **Open** Kodi and commence your media consolidation

Method #4: Using adbLink on your Computer

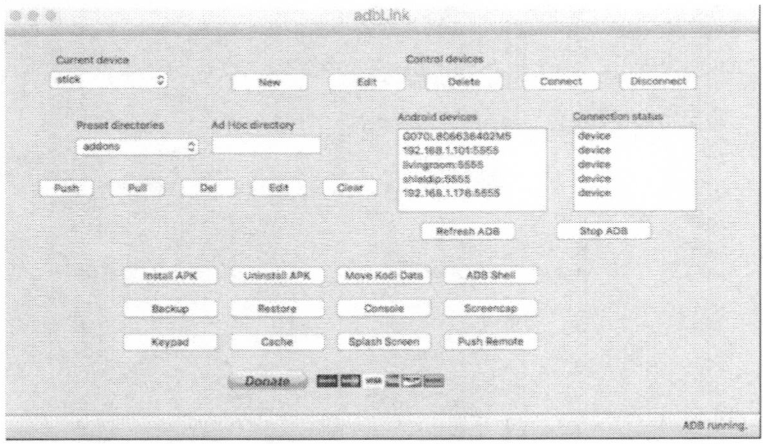

This method is utilized for Windows, Mac or Linux. The adbLink is a side load method for installing Kodi on Fire TV. It also enables you to install other apps as well. This will allow you to copy files to and from Kodi, backup Kodi, mount USB drives, and many other options as well. AdbLink is a companion program for Fire TV.

Detailed Description

Step#1: Hardware Setup

- The first thing to do is to make sure your Fire TV Stick is plugged into the HDMI port into your TV.
- Set it up as normal with your Amazon account.
- Make sure your Fire TV Stick is connected to the **same router** as your phone or tablet.

Step#2: Turn ON the Apps from Unknown Sources feature

- Go to Main Menu on the Left Hand Side

- Tap **Settings**
- Inside Settings Tap **System**
- Inside System Tap **Developer Options**
- Enable **ADB Debugging** and **Apps from Unknown Sources**

Step#3: Find the IP address of your Amazon Firestick/TV

- Inside System Tap **About**
- Inside About Tap **Network**
- Here you can see the **IP Address** for your device
- Note down this address as we are going to use it later.

Step#4: Turn OFF Collect App Usage Data feature

- Go to Main Menu on the Left Hand Side
- Tap **Settings**
- Inside Settings Tap **Applications**
- Disable **Collect App Usage Data**

Step#5: Install adbLink and Kodi on your Computer

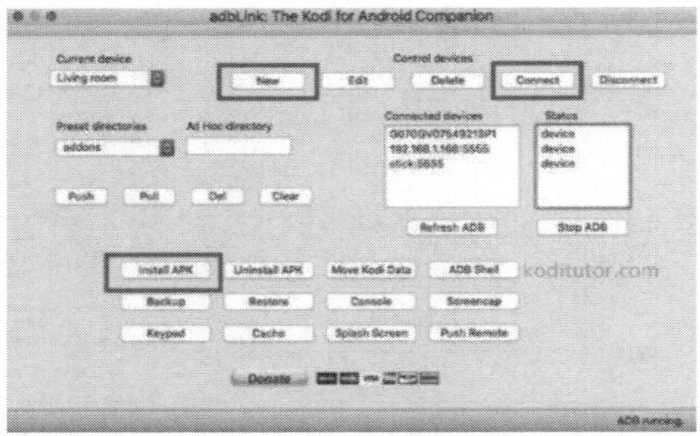

- Ensure that you are using the same **same router** as your Fire device
- Go to **kodi.tv** and click on the **Android APK ARM** option to **download** Kodi on your computer and save it.
- Go to **jocala.com** and find the download link for adblink
- **Download** the adblink for your Mac/PC/Linux OS and **install**
- Once adblink is installed you will see a page where you can add your Amazon Fire Device.
- On this page go to **Control Devices** section and tap **New**
- Here you will see a form that you need to fill
- In the **description** box type kodi
- In the **address** box type in the **IP address** that you got in Step#3 and it will connect your fire device to your adblink
- Now under the **Current Device** you can see kodi
- Go to **Control Devices** and tap **Connect**
- Once your device is connected, you can see your Amazon Fire device IP address in **connected devices** box and the **status** box saying device.

- Now tap the **Install APK** button, select the kodi file you had downloaded earlier and install the kodi on your adblink.
- Once the kodi installation is complete on adblink go to your Fire device and search for the installed kodi app
- Now you can **Open** Kodi and commence your media consolidation

After Installation

Now that you have Kodi on your Fire TV Stick, what do you do with it? The first thing to do is to go about adding some of those add-ons that we will talk about in the next chapter.

As a security measure, one of the things you are going to want to do is to run your Kodi through a Virtual Private Network (VPN). The most frequently mentioned way to do this is using a service called IPVanish. This is a paid service but for under $10 a month, this service hides your IP address and so allows you to access Kodi's content anonymously so that you don't need to worry about companies and hackers collecting your data. There are other side benefits to this service. The biggest is that it will prevent your Internet service provider (ISP) from throttling your connection, an especially important feature if you are using Kodi to play games.

Another is that since your IP address is hidden you are protected in case the government or a large corporation decides that the clips you've been watching on YouTube are now illegal. Other VPN services that are worth looking at include: NordVPN, Hide My Ass, Purevpn. Hotspot Shield, Vyprvpn, SAFERVPN, and HIDEme.

You will also want to install AppStarter, which will help you keep your Kodi updated. It doesn't do it automatically but it does check for the updates automatically and lets you install it with just one click.

Remote controls are one of the greatest inventions of the TV age. In fact, many features are designed specifically with remotes in mind. Kodi is no different and if you want to get the most out of it, it's recommended that you take the time to install Yatse.

This remote app can be downloaded straight from the Google Play Store and is considered by many to be the best Kodi remote out there. In addition to controlling the app and its many functions it also allows you to stream directly from your phone or tablet to your main Kodi device.

There are of course several kinds of remotes to try out. As with the install method, different remotes may be more effective depending on the generation of Fire TV Stick that you happen to own.

You may also want to check out Kore, Kodi's official remote app.

CHAPTER 4:

USING KODI ON YOUR FIRE STICK/TV

Basics of Kodi

Kodi is consistent across numerous operating systems. Kodi delivers a consistent experience and offers consistent features across a wide range of platforms. Kodibuntu, Android, iOS, Linux and Windows all have official versions of Kodi available.

- Due to its official support on most operating systems and hardware devices, Kodi does not require additional hardware or advanced hardware for installation and use on a TV.
- Kodi is multilingual and by default offers full support for many languages. Kodi is so adaptive that languages that are not available can be utilized by contacting the Kodi team. Languages that are already supported include languages as diverse as Afrikaans, Catalan, Finnish,

Maltese, Japanese, Turkish, Spanish, Basque, Icelandic and many others. A team of over 200 translators worked tirelessly to make Kodi available in 72 languages. More languages can be added at any time, by request.

Features

Kodi is a free, open source cross-platform media player for digital media, music and may other forms of content. It is officially available for many operating systems and is a native application that runs on most common processor architectures. Its ease of use and simple installation make it extraordinarily popular. It requires no additional hardware or advanced hardware to install.

As a media player and entertainment hub, it is unsurpassed in the industry. It can be used to play the latest audio and video formats, content that is stored to streamed, CDs, DVDs either directly from the source or stored. Multimedia can be streamed from anywhere in a residence or directly from the Internet. Kodi can be used to scan media to let you create a personal library. Weather, music, fan art, slideshows are available features of Kodi.

Menu

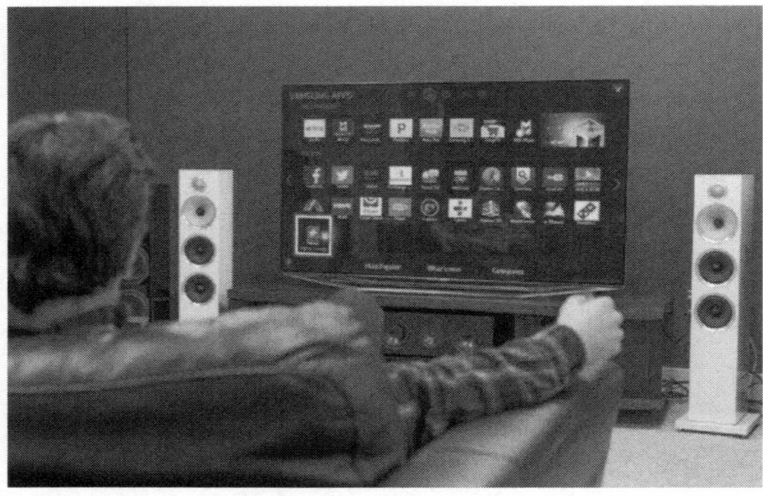

Kodi's interface is simple and you should try to familiarize yourself with it to get an idea of the uses you can get out it. If you open up the app on a computer, the program goes full screen, becoming the main interface for your system. Kodi's main menu has selections for a number of different media. These are as follows:

- Weather
- Pictures
- Videos
- Music
- Programs
- System

Each section also has sub-menus that appear when you highlight a given section. The selections in the submenu vary depending on whether or not you have any media added to them.

Taking the Music menu as an example, the submenu will allow you to access your music library according to Artist, Album and Track.

You can also go directly to the whole library and browse add-ons. Any albums recently added to your library will also be displayed (using any available artwork) above the menu bar in the top half of your screen.

When it comes to adding files to the menus, the process will be more or less cumbersome depending on how organized you are already. You simply browse your way to the relevant folder, name it whatever you want and add your files to it.

If you already have everything tucked away in appropriately labeled folders, this will be easy. If you are like me and have different albums, photos and other media stashed all over the place depending on where the files originally came from or what hobby you were into at the time, you might be tempted to think that the whole process is more trouble than it's worth. However, you only have to do it once and especially if you have a large collection, the initial tediousness will be more than worth the end result.

Music

Kodi can play your music in any format you desire. It can stream music or access stored content. Kodi can play AAC, MP3, FLAC, OGG, WAV and WMA file formats. Tagging support, cue sheet, and smart playlists give you control of your music and make it easy to access and organize.

Movies

Movies can be accessed in just about any format you can imagine. Formats that are accessible through Kodi include online media, ISOs, 3D, H.264, HEVC, and WEBM. Kodi can also import fan art, trailers, extras and much more.

TV Shows

Your favorite TV shows can be enjoyed through Kodi. It supports episodes, seasons, playlists, posters, show descriptions and every detail of your favorite TV Shows.

Unlimited Free Access

Using Kodi community developed add-ons, you have unlimited access to TV shows and movies.

PVR and Live TV

You can watch and record TV as you are watching it. This feature can be used from all GUI interfaces. It works with Media Portal, MythTV, NextPVR, Tvheadend, CVDR, and Windows Media Center.

Pictures

Using Kodi, you can import your pictures, sort, organize, filter and create slideshows. Add-ons. The add-ons available for Kodi are vast and cover many categories. This allows you to customize your media experience and enjoy Kodi any way you choose. The add-ons available are created by the Kodi community and include add-ons for videos, music, web services, weather, pictures and much more.

Skin

Using Kodi, you can change the entire GUI. You have the ability to change nearly every aspect of Kodi using the skinning engine. You can choose from community created skins or even create your own skin for a completely customized experience. UPnP. Kodi allows you to stream to and from other UPnP compatible devices in your home from your main entertainment hub, or master device. This allows you to import and synchronize the data inside your home between compatible devices. Web Interfaces. You can interact with Kodi using a remote interface. By utilizing a remote interface, you can add or customize 3rd party tools, web browsers and remote controls.

Remote Controls

You no longer have to rely on a TV remote, a DVD remote, and a universal remote to control the media in your home. With Kodi, you can now choose the way you control your media player and your Kodi experience, you can choose to use a traditional remote, or you can easily use your phone or tablet. In this book, there are instructions for setting up a phone or tablet as a remote control for Kodi.

CHAPTER 5:

EXPERIENCE KODI WITH ADDONS

There are literally dozens of decent media organizers on the market that will let you manage your files. So what makes Kodi so special? Kodi does so much more than provide a centralized location to manage the files that are already on your local network. It lets you add any kind of content from different sources and play it all on your TV.

This is where the many different add-ons come in. While there are hundreds to choose from, either by going through the app itself or going online to www.kodi.tv, not all of them were created equally. We'll be spending our time here going over some of the best and most popular add-ons. You will also get a demonstration of how to install these Addons to your Kodi.

Weather

There are only a handful of weather add-ons that are offered for Kodi, but let's face it; you only need one. The one that is most recommended (and that I use) is Yahoo! Weather. The app allows you to add multiple locations so you can see the weather where you are and where you are going to be, making it useful for planning activities during vacations. For those who just need a quick glance, handy graphics are provided that illustrates the forecast for the current day and the advance forecasts off to the side.

Other weather apps that are available are:

- **OpenWeatherMap Extended** – Lots of detailed info wherever you live.
- **Weather Underground** – This is a highly detailed app with local maps, radar and tons of data.

If you are not based in the US and would prefer to have something that is customized for your own country, there are a few options for you.

- **Met Office** – UK-centric weather.
- **Oz Weather** – For the land down under.
- **Weather China** – Pretty self-explanatory.

Skins

Don't like the default look of Kodi? Not to worry, there are a number of downloadable skins available that will let you completely change the look and feel of the app. Fair warning, many of these also change the interface so you may need to spend some time relearning how to interact with your program and find your files again.

Check the user reviews to find out if there are any problems with links and paths to your content getting broken by the skin you are looking at. And even if you happen to like the default skin for your Kodi, other skins might actually be better and open up more features for you.

To change your skin, you'll first need to download and/ or enable one or more skins to try out. To do that

- Go to **System** in the Main Menu
- Tap **Settings**
- Inside Settings tap **Appearance**
- Inside Appearance tap **Skins**
- Inside the Skins, tap **Get More** and proceed to select, download and explore different skins.

Below are some of the better skins available for Kodi:

- **Aeon Nox** – A good skin that makes it easy to read high contrast text.

- **<u>Amber</u>** – Provides customization options like customizing the home menu and background.
- **<u>Black Glass Nova</u>** – This gives you lots of widgets, artwork options and looks good on HD screens.
- **<u>Mimic</u>** – Clear, touch support, and even incorporates fan art.
- **<u>ReFocus</u>** – ReFocus provides many of the same features as other skins, with a design focus on sidebar menus and large, beautiful artwork.
- **<u>Eminence</u>** – There are not a lot of features in this one but it is very smooth operating and slick looking.
- **<u>Nebula</u>** – The design is a little messy but looks good in HD and has plenty of features to make up for its design faults.
- **<u>Xperience 1080</u>** – A good, full-screen app with a nice home menu. Unfortunately, it doesn't have a great deal of touch support.
- **<u>Transparency</u>** – An easy to use a skin that is a fan art friendly.
- **<u>Ace</u>** – This skin isn't bloated and yet somehow has tons of features.

Video Add-ons

The most popular and diverse add-ons for Kodi are those that allow you to stream video from a number of sources. You can find sources for your favorite content from live soccer to F1 from anywhere on the globe on all major networks.

That's the beauty of Kodi, content from round the world at your finger tips!

Due to the diverse a nature of these add-ons, we'll spend a bit more time with them than others. You will also learn how to install Exodus and IPTV to Kodi.

Exodus

By far the most popular Kodsi add-on is Exodus, a media scraper used to integrate content from providers all over the Internet. Exodus allows you to watch movies and TV from many different sources online. It will also collect metadata like runtimes and artwork for the content being brought to your device. For the first few clicks, the interface is nothing special, just a series of lists for different content. Once you narrow it down, though, things change dramatically.

You suddenly find your screen filled with art from many, many movies, or whatever content you are exploring. This is also where you can get into trouble. Exodus doesn't discriminate between legal and illegal feeds. So use careful judgment here when browsing through content. Personally, I will still find it useful to access content that I already own or is part of some service I already have an account for, as it makes it available all in one place.

It could also be useful for filling in gaps in network coverage if you live in a place that does not get a good broadcast signal.

Install Exodus on Kodi

- Open Kodi
- In the main menu go to **System**
- Inside the sub-menu, go to **File Manger**
- Inside the File Manager click on **Addsource**
- A window will popup, where you need to type http://fusion.tvaddons.ag/ in the text box.
- Next, it will ask you to give a name to this file, lets name it **Exodus** then press Ok
- Now, go back to the main menu and click on **System**
- Inside the sub-menu, go to **Settings**
- Inside the Settings page, go to **Add-ons**
- Inside the Add-ons page click on **Install from Zip file**
- Now you can see the file (Exodus) you had earlier downloaded, click on the **Exodus file**
- Next, click on **Kodi Repos**
- Inside the Kodi Repos, choose **English/International** depending on your language and click on your selection

- Now you can see a list of repository files, click on **repository.exodus-1.0.0.zip**
- The file download will start and you can see the status on the bottom right hand side
- Now, go back to **Add-Ons**
- Click on **Install from Repository**
- Next, click on **Exodus Repository**
- Inside the Exodus Repository click on **Video Add-on**
- Inside the Video Add-on, click **Exodus** and press the **install** button and installation will start
- Once installed you can access it in the Add-ons sub-menu of the Videos section
- Now you can start using it.

Install IPTV on Kodi

- Open Kodi
- In the main menu go to **System**
- Inside the sub-menu, go to **File Manger**
- Inside the File Manager click on **Addsource**
- A window will popup, where you need to type http://toptutorials.co.uk/kodi in the text box.
- Next, it will ask you to give a name to this file, lets name it **TT Repo** then press Ok
- Now, go back to the main menu and click on **System**
- Inside the sub-menu, go to **Settings**
- Inside the Settings page, go to **Add-ons**
- Inside the Add-ons page click on **Install from Zip file**
- Now you can see the file (TT Repo) you had earlier downloaded, click on the **TT Repo**
- Next, click on **Kodi Repos**

- Inside the Kodi Repos, choose **English/International** depending on your language and click on your selection
- Now you can see a list of repository files, click on **andy.repository.zip**
- The file download will start and you can see the status on the bottom right hand side
- Now, go back to **Add-Ons**
- Click on **Install from Repository**
- Next, click on **Andy Repository**
- Inside the Andy Repository click on **Program Add-ons**
- Inside the Program Add-on, click **Andy Maintenance** and press the **install** button and installation will start
- Once installed go to the main menu
- Click on **Programs**
- Inside the programs click on **Andy Maintenance**, here you can see loads of options.
- Click on **IPTV**, it will download the add-on.
- Once the download is complete, click on **Yes** to install
- Now, go back to the **main menu**
- Go to videos and click on **Add-ons**
- Here you can see a list of IPTV address that you can use to access live TV
- Now you can start using it.

Phoenix

Phoenix is very similar to Exodus. It accesses many of the same sources, but it has a few additional features that some will find useful, such as a kids section and an additional focus on finding media streams for sports. There is a heavy focus on soccer (or football, if you live outside the US) and hockey, with feeds available from games all over the world.

There are also feeds from various networks based in the United States like ABC and CBS. The interface is considerably less attractive than Exodus as it never gets beyond scrollable lists.

SportsDevil

Speaking of sports, SportsDevil has a number of channels for streaming but also includes live streams from other sources. Fair warning, though, if there a lot of people trying to stream at the same time, your feed will be a bit choppy. As with the other sports friendly apps, SportsDevil largely focuses on non-US sports like soccer. One great option I found in this one is a variety of sources for cricket. This is a personal favorite sport and it is very hard to find a source that actually plays cricket matches, so this app is great in that regard.

1Channel

If Exodus seems a little too busy and you would rather not have all of the extra data cluttering up your screen, then this is the add-on for you. 1Channel plays the same content as the larger, more popular platform, but without all the bells and whistles.

SALTS

Stream all the Sources. It provides you with numerous video sources, including paid and free sources. Naturally, the paid sources are more reliable, but you do not need to necessarily use them.

Whether you go for the paid or the unpaid, there are a lot of movies and TV shows from the US and international shows that are available – all you need to do is scroll.

cCloud TV

Yes, another TV app. This one though will be particularly useful for multilingual users as it focuses on streaming channels from all around the world. The interface on this one is almost backward from that of Exodus. You initially will find a number of thumbnails breaking the selections into different categories like Top 10, Sports, Movies, etc.

Once you are in the category, though, it becomes a list of available media sources. While there are many good sources in this add-on, I found many streams that did not work.

YouTube

YouTube is, of course, the number one source on the Internet for independently created video content of virtually any kind on the Internet. The Kodi add-on lets you easily browse through its hundreds of thousands (if not millions) of channels or focus only on the popular ones.

There is also a list of live streams that let you watch everything from live streams of earth from the International Space Station

(ISS) to news stations, eagle watching, and even a live view of Venice, Italy. Also included are live music streams and a beautiful replay of solar flares, which combined with the music the channels creator chose, is nothing short of entrancing.

SyFy

If you like the tongue in cheek fun of Z Nation or the modern day reboot of Van Helsing, then this add-on is for you.

Music Add-ons

Lest you come away from this thinking that Kodi is really only useful for online video, we should spend some time talking about some of the options for music. There are of course many different simple radio streams to choose from, allowing you to listen to stations from nearly any nation imaginable. There are other options, though, many of them already in the default add-on menu.

- **NPR** – An American listener-supported news organization.
- **SoundCloud** – A good source for finding independent music and other audio content.
- **Serial Podcast** – This podcast has gotten a great deal of notoriety for its long-form true stories told in a serialized format.
- **OneDrive** – This add-on allows you to access any audio content that you have loaded onto your Microsoft OneDrive.
- **Loyal Books** – There are over 7000 audiobooks from the public domain available in this add-on.

- **Apple iTunes Podcasts** – As one might expect, this allows you to access Apple's vast array of available podcasts. And you don't even need to download iTunes or have an account.

There are others that require going outside the default list but are well worth the extra trouble to install.

- **ITunes** – There is a good chance that you already have this on your phone. Put it on your Kodi so you can access all your favorite stations and not burn up any of your data when you're at home.
- **Spotify** – This streaming music service will require you to have an account but you can get all the latest music from pretty much any genre.
- **YouTube Music** – If you want to keep your music and cat videos separate, then this add-on is perfect for you.
- **Google Music** – Another paid service, but with plenty to choose from.
- **Vevo Music** – If you don't just want music, this one gives you HD music videos. It might help you remember why MTV stopped playing them all the time.

Install MP3 Stream Addon

- Open Kodi
- In the main menu go to **System**
- Inside the sub-menu, go to **File Manger**
- Inside the File Manager click on **Addsource**
- A window will popup, where you need to type http://fusion.tvaddons.ag/ in the text box.
- Next, it will ask you to give a name to this file, lets name it **MP3** then press Ok
- Now, go back to the main menu and click on **System**
- Inside the sub-menu, go to **Settings**
- Inside the Settings page, go to **Add-ons**
- Inside the Add-ons page click on **Install from Zip file**
- Now you can see the file (Exodus) you had earlier downloaded, click on the **MP3** file
- Next, click on **XBMC Repos**
- Inside the Kodi Repos, choose **English/International** depending on your language and click on your selection

- Now you can see a list of repository files, click on **repository.kinkin-1.4.zip**
- The file download will start and you can see the status on the bottom right hand side
- Now, go back to **Add-Ons**
- Click on **Install from Repository**
- Next, click on **Kinkin Repo**
- Inside the MP3 Stream click on **Music Add-on**
- Inside the Video Add-on, click **MP3 Stream** and press the **install** button and installation will start
- Once installed you can access it in the Add-ons sub-menu of the Music section
- Now you can start using it.

Games

Everyone loves games. But not everyone can afford the multi-hundred dollar systems that are at the cutting edge of gaming and the thought of another Candy Crush or Clash of Clans clone makes your skin crawl. You long for something in between.

Thanks to people who grew up with classic arcade games and had a bit of spare time on their hands, many of the games that paved the way for the immersive 3D games of today are available for free or at least at a very low cost on the Internet.

You will need to download and install whatever emulators you need to access the games you are interested in. There are emulators for all of the old Nintendo systems from the original to the legendary Nintendo 64. You can also get emulators for Atari and Sega (including Dreamcast) systems. For the older systems like NES and Atari, all the classic games will be playable. If you are looking for games from the newer systems like N64 and Dreamcast, the frame per second (fps) capabilities of the Fire TV Stick will be limiting. For example, the still very playable Goldeneye on N64 is not available to play on the tiny stick.

Some of the N64 games that will play are Starfox, MarioKart, Duke Nukem, Badland and Reaper.

If retro games are your primary concern, one of the best add-ons for you is the **Rom Collection Browser**. Found in Kodi's official repository of add-ons, this will let you play tons of classic games.

There are numerous configuration options as well. Depending on how much time you want to invest in it, you can choose games in a list, with artwork, or even video previews.

RetroArch is another excellent emulator. This one is massive, and while it can be a bit difficult to set up, it has support for tons of game systems from handheld systems like Nintendo 3DS and PlayStation Portable to consoles like PlayStation 3 and Nintendo Wii. Perhaps you are worried that you will need to play this with the Fire remote or your phone and that might be a little cumbersome.

Kodi Compatible Gamepads

Fortunately, there are gamepads that are compatible with Kodi

- **Playstation4 Dual Shock Bluetooth Controller**– This one works without any extensive configurations. Should be good for most games out of the box.
- **Ouya Bluetooth Gamepad**. Ouya has a long battery life and has been found to continue working well after several months of heavy use.
- **Red Samurai Bluetooth Game Controller**– This controller has a lot of good reviews and is compatible with the Fire TV Stick.
- **Amazon Fire TV Game Controller**-This is guaranteed to work and will be a good option that is cheap and sure to keep you gaming for a long time to come.
- **Nyko Playpad Pro**– There is a chance that it will work, but given that only a third had been reported to work it isn't recommended. Spend the extra money to get one of the above options and avoid this one like the plague.

Pictures

Like everyone, you have hundreds and thousands of photos that you've taken with your phone. And like everyone, they are scattered between different services and folders.

Kodi comes with many approved add-ons to finally get those things organized. Now you can browse them easily and display them on your big screen for everyone's enjoyment.

These include:

- **iPhoto** – Import all of your iPhoto events and albums.
- **Flickr** – Syncs with your Flickr account.
- **Photo app** – Import information from the OS X Photo App.
- **OneDrive** – Synchs with your OneDrive account.
- **DBMS** – Syncs with your Dropbox account.

There are plenty of other options as well. Entertainment options range from webcomics to slideshows, to aggregators. There are more serious options as well to help you search for images online and others collecting images from news sites around the web.

Comics

- **Dilbert** – Office comedy hilarity.
- **Garfield** – The original fat cat.
- **XKCD** – Humor for nerds who love math and language. I'm one of them.

Just for fun

- **Last.FM Slideshow** – This add-on displays a slideshow synced with whatever music you are already playing through one of your add-ons.

Image search and News

- **Google** – Search, view, and save images from around the Internet.

- **Zenfolio** – View and browse your gallery and other public galleries of photos.
- **The Big Picture** – Collection images from an array of sources from The Atlantic to The Wall Street Journal
- **500px** – A collection of various photos from cityscapes to cute and cuddly animals.

CHAPTER 6:

TROUBLESHOOTING AND MORE

Essential knowledge about any sort of software that you're planning on using is important. This chapter will deal with certain aspects of Kodi that you should know about to use it successfully.

We will also talk about certain disadvantages that come with Kodi and how you can overcome them. Also, you'll get some tips and tricks along with answers to common queries.

Tips, Tricks and Troubleshooting

Kodi Website

Before you begin the installation of Kodi on an Amazon Fire TV or Fire Stick, take some time to research Kodi to be sure that you are getting all the features and benefits that you want and that are available. You may be surprised to find out just how customizable Kodi truly is. Also, by familiarizing yourself with the available features and apps, you can truly make your experience using Kodi much more enjoyable.

Accessing the Kodi website is simple. You will need to know how to access this web page and how to find the download button and menu to install Kodi on your Fire TV. Getting to know the website is a good way to learn about the company, research the product and decide which features and add-ons that you want to include before you attempt to install Kodi on your Fire TV. On your computer, type in Kodi or Kodi.tv into your search engine. Kodi is so popular that it should be on the very first page of your search results.

Select Kodi.tv. The home page will include a menu bar across the top that includes the following menus: About, Download, Add-ons, Wiki, Forum, Donate, Contact and Get Involved. There are also Social media buttons located in the top right-hand corner.

On the right-hand side, you will see a dark gray download button. Make a note about the download menu and the button; you will need this information before you can install Kodi on your Fire TV. You can select the Download Menu button and get a good idea of the stable versions of Kodi that are available for your operating system.

To really see what Kodi has to offer you as a media player and platform, select the Add-ons button on the menu bar. When you select the button, you will immediately see the page that displays categories. By selecting any of the categories, you will be able to see all the available add-ons for Kodi. Click on any of these categories and you will be amazed at the selection of potential add-on you can access through Kodi.

Since Kodi is a nonprofit, you may be able to find helpful tips, suggestions troubleshooting information by selecting the Forum menu button on the menu bar at the top. You can access any information on the site as a guest, but you will need to sign in to post on a topic or answer any question.

Always back up

This is one of the most common downfalls and can save all of your settings and media in your library. Before downloading and installing Kodi, even in its stable version, it is always a good idea to back up files and settings. If you already have Kodi installed, backup all your settings and library before downloading and installing a new version.

Android

When installing Kodi using Android, here are a few tips that will help you avoid common difficulties: Make sure Kodi will work on your android device. Before purchasing an android device or any hardware for android, be sure that it will work for your device and is able to support Kodi add-ons and community developed apps.

Wi-Fi

Be sure you have access to a strong Wi-Fi signal. If you have weak Wi-Fi, it is best to avoid using wireless. You may have to use a USB Wi-Fi adapter. If you seem to have a networking issue, switch devices. Try media sharing on a different device if you have an issue with a specific device.

Speed

Disable RSS feed if it is enabled to improve main menu speed. Hi10P does not work on android. If you are having difficulty streaming a video that is H.264 it may be encoded with Hi10P. This may require a faster processor or you may not be able to stream these videos.

Visit the Kodi website for additional troubleshooting and installation help and video tutorials. Consult Kodi tech support on the Kodi website. Kodi does not have a customer support center, but they do have a community-supported forum available. As a guest, you can post questions regarding any issues you may have with your Kodi installation.

When in doubt consult the Internet. There are many great tutorials on installation and troubleshooting, which can help you easily avoid any potential issues.

Buffering

Sometimes your Kodi may just keep of buffering and not load a program/addon. This happens for various reasons and the best solution is to reboot your fire stick. To do this, first switch off your internet, then reboot the device.

No Volume

If you have volume issues on Kodi, check the volume amplification setting on your Kodi.

- Go to Settings
- Go to Volume
- Change the volume Setting
- Now go back and enjoy your content.

Repository Updates

The repositories need to be updated sometimes when it shows the add-ons empty or not functioning properly.

- Go to System
- Go to Settings
- Select Add-on
- Click Get Add-on
- Click on the repository that is troubling you and open the content box and check for updates.
- Once the updates are done, reopen the repository.

- Now it should work fine.

Settings and Configuration

Kodi is compatible with almost every operating system and interfaces easily with hundreds of devices, still, there can be occasional obstacles during installation.

In this section, you will learn ways to how to seek assistance if you run into issues.

Backup/Restore Kodi

- Use your search box on the Fire home screen to find ES

File Explorer

- Tap on the icon to download the App
- Launch the ES File Explorer App
- Go to ES File Explorer
- In the Main Menu on the ES File Explorer ensure that Show Hidden Files option is On
- Now, in the Main Menu go to Local
- Inside Local go to Home
- Look for the folder org.xbmc.kodi and click on it
- Go to the folder Files and click on it
- Here you can see the folder named .Kodi, select it and copy it.
- Now go back to Local and select Download
- Inside Download paste the .Kodi folder

Now all your addons and data are backed up. You can access this file and restore all the add-ons and data when ever you want. You can even transfer it on to another Fire Device.

Reload Kodi/Fresh Start

After using Kodi for a long time it becomes slow because all the media/content that we import makes the program very heavy. To overcome this, I usually do a Fresh Start so that all the cache is deleted and the system becomes lighter and faster. To execute fresh start on your Firestick follow these simple steps.

- Go to Firestick **Main Menu**
- Go to **Settings**
- Click on **Applications**
- Click on **Manage Apps**
- Click on **Kodi**
- Click on **Clear Data**

This is will execute the fresh start and you can begin fresh on your Kodi. However please remember that fresh start will delete all the data and you will need to reload everything once again.

Clearing Cache

If you don't want to execute a fresh start and struggling with a slow Kodi, its best to clear the cache and free up some space. This will lighten up your Kodi media center.

- Go to Programs in the Main Menu
- Go to Add-on
- Click on the Add-on installer
- Click on Program Add-on
- Click on Maintenance Tool
- Click Install and after its installed, click Ok
- Now, go back to Programs
- Click on Maintenance Tool and continue when prompted
- Click Ok and General Maintenance to continue

- Now, go to Clear Cache
- Click Ok

Now it will clear your cache and help run Kodi faster.

Removing Add-ons

Another reason your Kodi may become slow is too many add-ons. It's a good practice to periodically remove the add-ons you are not using. Doing so will not only help you with a better Kodi experience but also avoid piracy issues. Sometimes hackers use these add-ons to hack into your system and steal credit card details. So the rule of thumb is to uninstall the add-ons not being used. To execute an uninstall just follow this procedure.

- Go to System
- Click on Settings
- Click on Add-ons
- Click on the Add-on you want to remove
- Click on Uninstall.

That's it! You are done. The add-on is removed.

Upgrading Kodi

In the future when a new version of Kodi replaced the one that you have just installed, you will undoubtedly want to install it. Installing a new version is easy. Download the correct version of Kodi. Be sure that the ADB is connected to your Fire TV. Run the command adb install – r < apk-file-name >. When you see the word success, your installation is complete. Your settings will remain intact in the new version. You may see Kodi cycle through a first run screen, but your settings will still be there.

Disadvantages of Kodi

In recent years, Kodi has also been the subject of negative publicity and misinformation stemming from third party activity not related to the company.

Due to Kodi's compatibility with third party add-ons, there have been many cases of third party product developers and sellers marketing Kodi as an easy way to access pirated material. Kodi has vehemently condemned such practices. Unfortunately, Kodi's compatibility with almost any operating system, add on, or plugin has made it vulnerable to this type of illegal activity.

Kodi is categorized as a blank slate technology. What that means is that Kodi is not legally responsible for any illegal use of its media player by its users or third party sellers. This blank slate gives users nearly unlimited freedom to customize Kodi to fit their needs, unfortunately, it also allows for unlimited access by users who want to access unlicensed content.

Rather than change its product and restrict use or compatibility that would restrict users who are not trying to illegally access unlicensed content, Kodi has chosen to take a different strategy.

To distance itself from a brand name and a trademark from any and all illegal products or this practice, Kodi has systematically taken a public stance of denouncing this activity, while at the same time chosen to legally take an aggressive course of action. Aside from the unfortunate and unintended association with an illegal activity, Kodi has otherwise enjoyed a stellar reputation.

Amazon Fire Stick and Amazon TV have both benefited by their association with Kodi. Other operating systems and products have found similar success by advertising their compatibility with Kodi or packaged with Kodi already downloaded.

In 2014, XBMC won a Life Hacker Award for the best media player for entertainment. In 2006, 2007, and 2008 XBMC won the Sourceforge Community Choice Awards.

CONCLUSION

Kodi is a free media center that has enjoyed unrivaled popularity. The product offered by Kodi is adaptable, customizable and compatible with nearly every operating system in current use. It has been widely regarded as a reputable product that offers many desirable features and benefits.

Kodi is a free, open source cross-platform media player for digital media, music and may other forms of content. It is designed to operate as an entertainment for your home theater. Kodi allows you to easily access videos, movies, music, podcasts, the Internet and many other sources of content with a remote control. Mobile phones can be utilized to act as remote controllers input, access and control of Kodi.

The Amazon Fire Stick and TV are both ingenious products that you can use with Kodi to change the interface of your Smart TV and make it a consolidated media hub.

Kodi has multiple uses and you will only learn to use it with time. I hope that this book was informative and helped you to understand your Fire TV better.

Did you Like this Book?

Let everyone know by posting a review on Amazon. Just click here and it will take you directly to the review page.

And if want to learn some real DIY hack on your new Amazon Echo do get in touch at kindletechgames@gmail.com

YOU MAY ALSO LIKE

Amazon Echo Advanced User Guide

Amazon Echo Dot Advanced User Guide

Kindle Fire HD 8 & 10

Advanced User Guide

Releasing Soon

Amazon Alexa

Advanced User Guide

APPENDIX

Made in the USA
Lexington, KY
25 April 2017